STORIES OF
PERSISTENCE

SOCIAL EMOTIONAL LIBRARY

CHERRY LAKE
Publishing

Published in the United States of America by Cherry Lake Publishing
Ann Arbor, Michigan
www.cherrylakepublishing.com

Content Adviser: Satta Sarmah Hightower, www.sattasarmah.com
Reading Adviser: Marla Conn MS, Ed., Literacy specialist, Read-Ability, Inc.

Photo Credits: ©Jupiterimages/Thinkstock Images, cover, 1; ©dragon_fang/Shutterstock Images, 5; ©PD-US, 7; ©Newsweek/ Wikimedia, 8; ©Walter Lantz Productions/Wikimedia, 11; ©Wikimedia, 12; ©Jerry Coli/Dreamstime Images, 15; ©ARENA Creative/Shutterstock Images, 16; ©Jerry Coli/Dreamstime Images, 17; ©mTaira/Shutterstock Images, 18; ©Daniel Ogren/ Flickr, 21; ©Lucy Clark/Shutterstock Images, 22; ©Simon Davis/DFID/Wikimedia, 25; ©JStone/Shutterstock Images, 27; ©Obama White House/Flickr, 28

Library of Congress Cataloging-in-Publication Data
Names: Colby, Jennifer, 1971- author.
Title: Stories of persistence / by Jennifer Colby.
Description: Cherry Lake Publishing : Ann Arbor, [2018] | Series: Social emotional library |
    Audience: Grade 4 to 6. | Includes bibliographical references and index.
Identifiers: LCCN 2017033505 | ISBN 9781534107410 (hardcover) | ISBN 9781534109391 (pdf) |
    ISBN 9781534108400 (pbk.) | ISBN 9781534120389 (hosted ebook)
Subjects: LCSH: Life skills—Juvenile literature. | Empathy—Juvenile literature.
Classification: LCC HQ2037 .C643 2018 | DDC 646.7—dc23
LC record available at https://lccn.loc.gov/2017033505

Cherry Lake Publishing would like to acknowledge the work of The Partnership for 21st Century Learning.
Please visit www.p21.org for more information.

Printed in the United States of America
Corporate Graphics

ABOUT THE AUTHOR

Jennifer Colby is a school librarian in Michigan. She has persisted throughout the years in order to earn the college degrees necessary for her career.

TABLE OF CONTENTS

CHAPTER 1

What Is Persistence?

Have you ever not done well the first time you tried something? Maybe you couldn't play an instrument very well or you could not run as fast as others. Or maybe someone told you that you were not good at singing or at math? Did you give up right away, or did you keep trying? If you kept trying, then you were persistent. Persistence is a trait that makes it possible for someone to keep doing something even though it is difficult or opposed by other people. There are many people throughout history who have exhibited persistence in their lives.

Being persistent has its rewards.

CHAPTER 2

Thomas Edison

Have you ever watched a movie, listened to music, or flipped a switch to turn on a light? Do you know who invented the things that enable these actions? It's the "Wizard of Menlo Park," Thomas Alva Edison. With 1,093 US **patents** to his name, Edison invented many of the devices that helped develop our society. But life was not easy for Edison. He faced challenges that developed his strong sense of persistence.

Born in Ohio on February 11, 1847, Thomas Alva Edison had many setbacks in his 84 years before achieving success. Edison did not learn how to speak until he was four years old. By age seven, after only 12 weeks of school, he came home with a note from his teacher that said Edison was not smart enough to learn. Today, he would probably have been diagnosed with

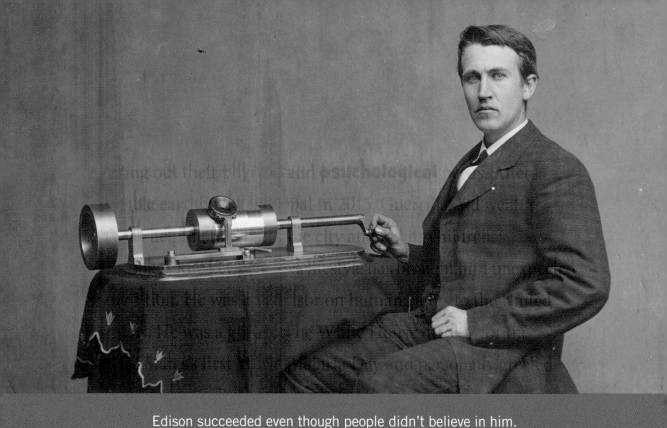

Edison succeeded even though people didn't believe in him.

attention-deficit/hyperactivity disorder (ADHD). His mother read the note and decided to teach Edison herself.

From the age of 12, Edison had many jobs to earn money for his struggling family and to engage his curious mind. He sold newspapers on the local railroad, eventually publishing his own newspaper. During his youth, Edison caught **scarlet fever**, which many believe worsened his lifelong hearing difficulties. He was later banned from selling newspapers on the train when his trunk full of chemicals exploded and set a train car on fire. By age 15, he left home to seek his fortune working as an **itinerant telegraph** operator.

The Edison Mazda Lamps were named in his honor.

During this time, he developed a device that allowed anyone to easily and correctly translate **Morse code** signals as it sent them between telegraph stations. He never profited from his automatic repeater device. Later he created an electric vote-counting machine, but this invention was a total disaster. He was unable to market it to anyone because, at that time, elected officials depended on the slow process of hand counting votes. The extra time this involved allowed candidates to try and sway those who had not yet voted.

[21ST CENTURY SKILLS LIBRARY]

After being fired from Western Union for devoting too much time to outside interests, Edison moved to New York City and soon invented the Universal Stock Printer. This device modernized the **stock exchange** and earned him $40,000. With this money, Edison set up a factory in Newark, New Jersey, in 1871. He moved to Menlo Park in 1876 and opened the first modern research lab. Now he could devote his life to full-time inventing.

Perhaps Edison's greatest invention of all, the electric light bulb, best displays his persistence. He worked on developing the light bulb for more than 10 years before he finally succeeded. He stated, "I have constructed three thousand different theories in connection with the electric light … yet only in two cases did my experiments prove the truth of my theory." Later, while developing a battery for Henry Ford's new automobile, Edison was asked by a reporter about his results, which were a failure at that point. He responded, "Results! Why, man, I have gotten lots of results! I know several thousand things that won't work!"

One of the simple principles Edison followed was, "Never get discouraged if you fail. Learn from it. Keep trying." This persistence in life helped him to work past setbacks and failures in order to become one of the most **prolific** inventors of the industrial age.

Walt Disney

You've heard of Disneyland or Disney World and watched Disney movies, but did you know that only one man made these things possible? Walt Disney is still regarded as one of the most successful men in the entertainment business, but he suffered many failures throughout his career. He never gave up, though. This attitude, which brought him a lot of success, is proof that persistence pays off.

Born in Illinois on December 5, 1901, Disney's family soon moved to Missouri where Walt sold pictures that he drew to neighbors and friends. He loved trains and had a summer job selling snacks and newspapers to passengers on a train. While attending high school in Chicago, Illinois, he was a cartoonist for his school's paper and he went to night classes at the Art Institute of Chicago.

During World War I, at age 16, he dropped out of high school to join the Army. But he was rejected for being too young and

In one of Oswald the Lucky Rabbit's adventures, he makes a mechanical turtle work.

instead joined the Red Cross. Then, they sent him to France to drive an ambulance. When he returned, he pursued a career as a newspaper cartoonist in Kansas City, Missouri, but was later fired for "not being creative enough." He began experimenting with hand-drawn **cel animation** and created his own cartoon animation business. But by 1923, his company ran out of money.

He and his brother Roy pooled their remaining money and moved to Hollywood, California. There they created a popular character named Oswald the Lucky Rabbit. But later Walt found out that his **distributor** had stolen the rights to Oswald as well as taken all of his animators. Disney's studio was failing—until

Disney's 1937 film *Snow White and the Seven Dwarfs* was a huge success.

he introduced the first talking cartoon called *Steamboat Willie*. Movie sound had just been invented, and Walt voiced the character of Mickey Mouse. It was a success.

In 1929, Disney's studio developed many popular animated cartoons that introduced the characters of Minnie Mouse, Donald Duck, Goofy, and Pluto. Even during the Great Depression, Disney's new full-length animated movie *Snow White and the Seven Dwarfs* was extremely popular. It made almost $3.5 million (in the US alone) and earned an Academy Award.

With this success, Disney opened a larger studio. But within a few years, the studio produced the box office failures *Pinocchio* and *Fantasia*. As a result, by 1941, Disney's employees were unhappy with the way the struggling business was run. Most of the animators went on **strike** and eventually quit their jobs. It would be many years before the company recovered.

The success of full-length animated films such as *Cinderella* and *Sleeping Beauty* helped Disney bounce back. He began to expand his animation company into an entertainment business and opened Disneyland in Anaheim, California, in 1955. The grand opening, though, was a disaster. Fake tickets, traffic backups seven miles (11 kilometers) long, rides that didn't work, melting pavement, and a shortage of food and water on a day when it was 100 degrees Fahrenheit (38 degrees Celsius) all disrupted the launch of the new theme park. "Probably for the first time in his career," reported the press, "Disney disappointed thousands of youngsters." Disney and his employees worked hard to get everything up and running smoothly within a couple of months. Disneyland was ultimately a success.

Despite multiple setbacks in his life, Walt Disney showed persistence. He won the most Academy Awards for his animated and live-action films. He also eventually opened many other theme parks around the globe.

Michael Jordan

Have you ever tried out for a team and didn't make it? Were you discouraged? Maybe it would encourage you to know that the greatest basketball player of all time was cut from his high school's varsity team. That player is Michael Jordan, and during his outstanding professional career, he won six NBA championships and two Olympic gold medals.

Michael Jordan was born February 17, 1963, in Brooklyn, New York. The fourth of five children, Jordan soon moved to Wilmington, North Carolina, where he attended Laney High School. In 1978, he was cut from the varsity basketball team during his sophomore year. At 5 feet 10 inches (178 centimeters), he was told he was too short to play on the team. Despite this, he played on the junior varsity team that year and had multiple 40-point games.

Jordan is no longer "too short" – he's 6 feet and 6 inches (198.12 cm) tall.

Driven to make the varsity team the next year, he trained hard. "Whenever I was working out and got tired and figured I ought to stop, I'd close my eyes and see that list in the locker room without my name on it," Jordan explained. "That usually got me going again." He had a 4-inch (10-cm) growth spurt and made the varsity cut during his junior year. He averaged 20 points per game and in his senior year was selected to the McDonald's All American Team.

Failing teaches us how to do better next time.

He was **recruited** by multiple colleges and ended up playing basketball for the University of North Carolina. He had a very successful college basketball career and was selected to the NCAA All-American First Team in both his sophomore and junior years. This caught the eyes of scouts working for professional teams. When the Chicago Bulls drafted him, Jordan left college before graduating. He later returned to the University of North Carolina to earn his degree in geography.

Jordan was a five-time NBA Most Valuable Player.

Jordan played minor league baseball for the Chicago White Sox.

Many professional athletes do not have successful careers, but because of his persistence and love of competition, Michael Jordan became talented at professional basketball and also baseball. After playing for the Chicago Bulls from 1984 to 1993 and winning three NBA championships, Jordan retired from basketball, saying he had lost his desire to play the game. He soon began playing minor league baseball. A year later, however, a players' strike put his baseball career on hold, and he returned to playing basketball with the Bulls.

Over the next four years, he led the team to three more NBA championships. In 1999, Jordan decided to retire again—but again he could not stay away from basketball for long. He became part owner of the Washington Wizards, and in 2001 began playing for the team. That same year, he donated his entire salary to the victims of the attacks on September 11, 2001.

Michael Jordan has said, "I've missed more than 9,000 shots in my career. I've lost almost 300 games. Twenty-six times I've been trusted to take the winning shot and missed. I've failed over and over and over again in my life. And that is why I succeed." Despite retirements and personal challenges, Jordan persisted, and he believes his failures are responsible for his success.

Are You Persistent?

When things get hard, do you give up easily or do you keep trying? If you keep trying, then you might be persistent. To be persistent means to keep doing things over and over again in order to get better, to create something, or to make sure that something can be done.

J. K. Rowling

Have you ever thought that you would like to become an author? Writing a book is harder than you think. J. K. (Joanne) Rowling is the author of the hugely successful Harry Potter books, but her success was not overnight. She once said that she was as "poor as it is possible to be ... without being homeless." But her persistence helped her to overcome many challenges in life and become one of the richest women in the world.

Rowling was born in Yate, England, on July 31, 1965. As a young child, she often wrote **fantasy** stories to share with her younger sister, though her parents never encouraged her to be a writer. Rowling's teenage years were unhappy. Her mother suffered from **multiple sclerosis**, and she had a strained relationship with her father. In 1982, Rowling applied to Oxford

In five years, Rowling went from being jobless to being a millionaire.

College, but failed the entrance exams and was not accepted. She instead went to the University of Exeter and studied French and classical studies.

While on a train trip in 1990, Rowling was inspired to write a story about a boy attending **wizardry** school. She returned home and began writing the story right away, but unfortunately, her mother died before Rowling had a chance to tell her about Harry Potter. She has said that her mother's death had a big influence on her writing, especially in the first book about Harry's feelings about the death of his parents.

The Wizarding World of Harry Potter is a theme park based on Rowling's books.

Soon after her mother's death, Rowling moved to Portugal to take a job as an English teacher and focus on completing her **manuscript**. While there, she got married and had a child. The marriage did not work out and, after separating from her husband, Rowling moved to Scotland with her infant daughter and only three finished chapters of her book. Without a job and with a child to care for, she considered herself a failure. And yet, Rowling found her situation freeing, and she used the extra time she now had to focus on writing while her daughter napped.

In 1995, Rowling sent her completed manuscript for

Harry Potter and the Philosopher's Stone to 12 different publishers. Each one rejected it. Rowling was advised to not quit her day job because she would never make any money as a children's author, but eventually a publisher finally accepted her manuscript. The book was published in 1997 and soon won the British Book Award for Children's Book of the Year. An American publisher bought the rights to the book and changed the title to *Harry Potter and the Sorcerer's Stone*. Rowling regretted the change and wished she could have prevented it.

Still, the success of the first book spurred her to continue writing the seven-volume series. Including books, movies, theme parks, and merchandise, Harry Potter is a global brand worth more than $25 billion. The last four books in the series set records for the highest book sales in history. Rowling has donated millions of dollars to charity and established her own charitable trust, which funds causes that are close to her heart. She has not forgotten the troubles she had in life and works to support the poor and children at risk.

In a 2008 speech to Harvard University graduates, Rowling admitted, "By every usual standard, I was the biggest failure I knew." J. K. Rowling persisted through poverty and rejection to become one of the best-selling fiction authors of all time.

Malala Yousafzai

In most countries, people expect that both boys and girls will go to school. But in some countries, political beliefs, religions, and poverty can deny girls an education. Malala Yousafzai lived in one of these countries. Many times, Malala was threatened, but she persisted in attending school because she believed in the value of an education.

Malala was born in Pakistan on July 12, 1997. Her mother and father ran a chain of schools. In the Swat Valley, where she lived, the **Taliban** forbade girls from attending school. The group believed that educating girls was a crime. After frequent Taliban attacks at girls' schools in her region, Malala gave a public speech called, "How dare the Taliban take away my basic

Malala is a survivor: she is persistent and courageous.

right to education?" Many newspapers and television channels in the area covered her speech. Later that year, she became a blogger for the **BBC** and wrote about her daily life. She never used her name, but her stories reached thousands of people around the world and brought awareness to the situation.

In January 2009, the Taliban legally prohibited all girls from attending schools. To enforce this policy, the group destroyed many schools. Many people in Malala's hometown felt uneasy and people were afraid to even leave their homes. Soon a peace deal was reached between the government and the Taliban. Girls were allowed to go to schools with boys, but the girls-only schools remained closed.

After a few weeks, girls' schools were allowed to reopen, and although the area was still being bombed, Malala was able to finish her exams. Then, a reporter from the *New York Times* interviewed Malala and her father on television. When the Pakistan Army moved into the region in May to push the Taliban out, Malala and her family were forced to move and Malala's family was separated. She went to live with relatives in the country, and her father went to the region's capital to **lobby** for support.

Persistence in the Workplace

Persistence is important when it comes to having a successful career. Even now, you're persisting toward your future—you're working hard at school so you can work wherever you decide. Refusing to give up makes all of your effort and work worthwhile. Persistence helps people achieve their goals, and it makes them feel accomplished and happy. If you work to overcome a difficult problem at work, you'll become more experienced and able to better handle similar problems in the future.

Malala attends the 2013 *Glamour* Woman of the Year Awards.

Malala meets President Barack Obama and his family.

Malala was shown in several televised interviews, and her identity as the BBC blogger was revealed. This enraged the Taliban. It had already made death threats against Malala's father, but in 2012 Taliban leaders agreed that Malala should be killed. By this time, she was nominated for the International Children's Peace Prize and the National Youth Peace Prize. At the young age of 15, her persistence in speaking out for girls' rights had made her a target of the Taliban.

On October 9, 2012, a Taliban gunman shot Malala. She was treated at an English hospital and recovered from her severe injuries a few months later. Since then, Malala has never returned home—she never can. The Taliban still **condemns** her.

Despite this threat, Malala has continued to campaign for the education rights of girls. Her efforts earned her a 2014 Nobel Peace Prize. Through great suffering, persistence, and determination, Malala received an education in a country that made it difficult for girls to do so. And she continues to speak out for girls around the world.

What Have You Learned About Persistence?

Persistence is hard work. It means not giving up when you want to. It means doing hard things when it would be easier not to. A common trait of many famous people is persistence—they never gave up until they achieved their goal. With commitment and persistence, you can achieve any goal, despite any challenges or obstacles you may come across along the way.

Think About It

How Can You Become More Persistent?

You can become more persistent by not giving up. When things get hard, take a deep breath and think about your goal. What are you trying to achieve? What is the best way to achieve it? If your goal is important enough to you, then you will be able to keep going for it.

For More Information

Further Reading

Krasniewicz, Louise. *Walt Disney: A Biography.* Santa Barbara, CA: Greenwood, 2010.

Lazenby, Roland. *Michael Jordan: The Life.* New York: Little, Brown and Company, 2014.

Yousafzai, Malala. *I Am Malala: The Girl Who Stood Up for Education and Was Shot by the Taliban.* New York: Little, Brown, and Company, 2013.

Websites

J. K. Rowling—About
https://www.jkrowling.com/about/
Visit J. K. Rowling's official website to learn more about the author.

Thomas A. Edison: Edison Innovation Foundation—All About Tom
https://www.thomasedison.org/all-about-tom
Read a biography of Thomas Edison.

GLOSSARY

BBC (BEE-BEE-SEE) the British Broadcasting Corporation, a media organization based in London

cel animation (SEL an-uh-MAY-shuhn) a series of hand-drawn cartoons put together to imitate movement

condemns (kuhn-DEMZ) says in a strong way that someone is wrong or should be punished

distributor (dih-STRIB-yuh-tur) a person who buys products from one company and arranges for other companies to sell them

fantasy (FAN-tuh-see) a story with magical or strange characters, places, or events

itinerant (eye-TIN-ur-uhnt) moving from place to place

lobby (LOB-ee) to try to influence government officials to make decisions for or against something

manuscript (MAN-yuh-skript) the original copy of a book before it has been printed

Morse code (MORS KOHD) a communication system that uses light or sound in patterns of dots and dashes to represent letters and numbers

multiple sclerosis (MUHL-tuh-puhl skluh-ROH-sis) a disease of the nervous system that causes the gradual loss of muscle control

patents (PAT-uhnts) official documents that give a person or company the right to be the only one that makes or sells a product for a certain period of time

prolific (pruh-LIF-ik) producing a large amount of something

recruited (rih-KROOT-ed) asked to join something

scarlet fever (SKAHR-lit FEE-ver) a very serious disease that causes a fever, sore throat, and a red rash

stock exchange (STAHK eks-CHAYNJ) a place where people buy and sell investments in companies

strike (STRIKE) a situation in which employees refuse to work until their demands are met

Taliban (TAHL-ih-bahn) a terrorist group that unlawfully uses threats and violence, especially against civilians, in order to gain power

telegraph (TEL-ih-graf) an old-fashioned system of sending messages over long distances by using wires and electrical signals

wizardry (WIH-zur-dree) the art or practice of magic

INDEX